Steel Valley

Michael Adams

LUMMOX Press

Illustrations by Raindog

ISBN 978-1-929878-17-8

First edition

LUMMOX Press
PO Box 5301
San Pedro, CA 90733
www.lummoxpress.com

Printed in the United States of America

Acknowledgments

My thanks to the editors of the following publications, in which these poems first appeared: Monongahela in *Desert Shovel Review;* Ghosts, and Like Old Buicks in *Mad Blood;* Headwaters in *Heartlodge;* Sweet, God's Son Lay Down and Autumn Night: Cold Mountain in *Heavy Bear*

For my grandparents
Michael Guydosh, Anna Lozko
Andrew Adamis, Anna Havrilla

You were the first generation
and laid the foundations.

Steel Valley

Contents

Introduction

In complex times, complexity becomes enshrined. Government gets bigger. Laws multiply. And often the people get hookwinked into voting against their own self-interest by the capitalist class of corporate mercantilists. Even the arts become a secret code, and avant garde poetry becomes accessible only to scholars and fellow poets.

Michael Adams is a poet of the people. He has a story to tell. From today and half a century ago. And he wants to communicate it with working class citizens, not just some ivory-towered literati. To do that, he employs a full range of genres in this crossover book— crafted lyrics, prose poems, field notes, bar talk, letters, haiku, recipes. Whatever it takes to share the tale.

His tone is consistent throughout— reflective and personal. It's clear Mike's chosen the bardic stance of Whitman, the nature zen of Snyder and the native spoken English of Lew Welch. No secret codes here. What you see is what you get. A man of the people speaking steel— memories and flashbacks, soliloquies and history.

In these perilous times, as empire and the world order, shift on their tectonic plates, it's good to remember where we have come as a people, as a nation. Mike takes us back to the steel heartland of America and forward to his life in the Rockies, and all of it flows like a river of molten metal.

Sit still for a moment and step into Pittsburgh's steel valley, as the grandson of a Hunky rabble-rouser on one side of the family and a bottom of the ladder company man on the other vie for the reader's sympathies. Some pieces will mystify you, as only good writing can. There will be leaps in time and space. The union man will rant against the bosses, injustice, and talk of a new old path, deeper than before. The company man will wax nostalgic for what's gone and offer glimpses of the raw beauty at the forged heart of industry. But despite the competing pulls, Mike's message is a simple one— tempered in the mills of Pennsylvania and nurtured in the nature of Colorado and West Virginia. It's what Dolores LaChapelle called The Way of the Mountain.

Mike was born at the peak of America's post-World War II prosperity, into what Norwegian eco-philosopher Sigmund Kvaloy has called "Industrial Growth Society." Now, having chosen the Chinese sage Crazy Cloud as his cross-generational mentor, he lives in Colorado, keeping a summer cabin/retirement home in the Wet Mountains.

His is a voice of passion, fierce truth and compassion for all beings. If you're lucky, you'll get to hear him read in that prophetic, incantatory style of a Homer or a Ginsberg. But whether you experience these pieces in person or in print, have a listen.

Here is a man who speaks to us from his heart, but cannot forget the lessons of intellect he's learned and wants to share. A man of the people.

—Art Goodtimes

I love poetry that illuminates the soul's travelogue. You can feel with all senses the steel wheels of Mike Adams' Pennsylvania steel mill and railroad boyhood pulse in every word; his clear, generous breaths open the heart to the wide expanses of the poet writing down his life. These tough, tender-eyed poems and prose pieces are at once blue collar and bohemian, homages to the drinking and the working life juxtaposed against a long poem about cooking green chili. There are disappearing riprap trails and epic family narratives that haunt and exhilarate. It is hard to find a geography worth its weight in memory that doesn't resonate with the blood and spirit of its inhabitants. Mike, like Ed Abbey before him, left behind the Wobbly Joe bars, mills, hills and scarred valleys of Pennsylvania for the boisterous outback of the comparatively wide, wild open West. *Steel Valley* is fine writing, epic and intimate.

—John Macker

*Who are you indeed who would
talk or sing to America?*
                    —Walt Whitman

Steel Valley

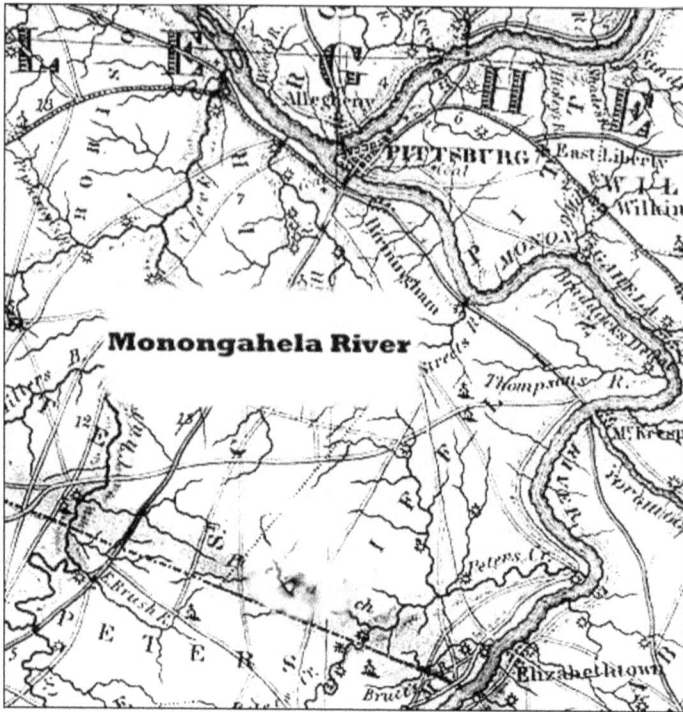

Monongahela

Looking back now, forty years gone,
my lack of curiosity about the river
I lived with daily disappoints me.

Maybe that's the way of youth,
to be fixated on origins and ends –
things far off, the cold mountain spring,
the distant sea, not the everyday.

The river itself, a slow brown ox,
harnessed to the yoke of industry,
was as common as my neighbors
and as of as little interest.

I carried with me in those days, before life touched me
with failure
and some sympathy, the hard stone of intolerance that
the young may bear
for the familiar, to mask their fear and uncertainty.

From the bluffs above Lock and Dam #2
I watched the tugs push their coal barges downriver,
imagined the days and nights of their long journeys,
past Pittsburgh, down the Ohio to the soft-banked Mississippi,
past all the towns with their wonderful sounding names —
Gallipolis, Oceola, Tallulah —

Dreamed of the bayous and salt-washed rivers,
sea-tangled with life —
ibises and spoonbills startling
the cypress swamps —
and the hot green cities –
Baton Rouge, New Orleans —
copper-haired women, skin sheened with sweat,
and the ice-hot wail of a saxophone
calling down heaven.

The Soft Fires

I stepped into the fires in the cathedral shadows of the furnaces,
in thrall to a life alloyed of iron and flesh.

It was Pittsburgh where I was tested and tempered,
Pittsburgh that entangled within me the chained indifferent fury
of industry and the unquenchable drives of the heart.

Our first time was in her second floor apartment
in South Oakland, where the city tumbles
down the bluff through blown trash
and woodland to the furnaces of Hazelwood.

The house was tumbling too, but slowly,
succumbing to gravity and the landlord's indifference
to paint, caulk and shingles. We didn't care, we

Were young, newly free, had lightning
on our minds. The maintenance of structures or love
meant nothing. Her bed was a jumble of Indian blankets
beneath bay windows that had resigned
the battle against wind and rain, leaving
long streaks of rust in the mustard yellow walls,
flecks of plaster on the sheets and a persistent smell of mold.

Ah, but that night –
there was a red glow
in the belly of the clouds from the furnaces, rain
hammered the windows and the October branches
of the sycamore battered the house.

I tasted the wind and rain and the sulphur grit
of the mill as I entered the fires and found her rhythm,
and we rocked together, welded by our hunger.

Michael Adams

The storm's thunder mixed with a deeper sound,
striking through the earth from the mill,
felt more than heard, some great machine
forming and shaping the bones of our city,
a monster hammering
deep in the soil and rock.

The night, our city

beautiful
molten
riven to the core.

STEEL VALLEY

Steel

I grew up in the Steel Valley, along the Monongahela River south of Pittsburgh. I'd lived all my life with the mills; steel ran in the blood of almost everyone I knew. So when I had a chance at a job there after my first year of college, I didn't have to think twice. I got hired into the blast furnaces at the Duquesne Works of US Steel, was put on the furnace crew after my first week. Third helper. Monkey Boss they called it, low man on the totem pole, but better than common laborer. Being on the crew, I knew where I was going every day when I reported for work, and I got bonus pay when we poured over our quota of iron. And we poured a lot of iron. The country was in high gear. Guns and butter, Vietnam and Johnson's Great Society. And I worked on Dorothy, the biggest furnace in the valley.

We poured a river of iron that ran through that hot Pittsburgh summer. Double shifts, 100 degree heat, protest marches, riots. Work like hell to get out one more cast. The base pay was for books, the bonus money for beer.

Iron ran an endless river. Five, six times a shift the warning came over the loudspeakers:

Hot metal! Yardmaster! Boilerhouse! Blast furnace clerk!

Number six is casting!

And there we'd stand in our big aluminum and asbestos furnace suits — moon walkers in a land as alien as any scorched cinder orbiting the edge of a star — and burn out the clay plug that held back the flood. The iron came out so hot it peeled the skin right off your nose through the faceplate. A hundred, hundred and twenty tons per cast, six, seven hundred tons a shift.

Iron ran an endless river – to railroad cars, rolling mills, tanks, Camaros, refrigerators, machine guns. It was a river that ran while King and Kennedy were killed. A river that ran through the guns of the soldiers – kids like me – who patrolled the streets of my hometown while the ghettos burned. A river that ran in a bloody stream stretched halfway round the world to sear the flesh of men and women I would never know, but start another river running, redder and hotter than molten steel.

And it was good old American steel for America's war. For American industry. For a country on a roll, heading for a fall but enjoying the ride. Not quite an honest day's pay for an honest day's work, an honest pitcher or two of Rolling Rock with my buddies at Chiodo's Tavern after work.

****

Mom's dad lost a leg in the mills before he was thirty, crushed by the steel wheels of a locomotive. He spent the rest of his working life as a clerk in the company office. Never made as much as the guys on the shop floor but kept his job through the depression and all the recessions and strikes and lay-offs right up to the day he retired.

Dad's dad was a union man — "goddam Hunky troublemaker"—to the Germans and Irish in the strike of 1919 — and died long before I was born. They lived in a shack down on the flats, just a block from US Steel's Homestead Works. One Saturday during the strike, so

the family story goes, the *Black Cossacks* came in on
horseback, right up the steps and through the door.
Got tangled in the laundry grandma had hanging in the
kitchen, which gave granddad just enough time to jump
out the window and hop a freight to Cleveland.

****

Orange clouds of sulfur off the slag pits, the stench of
rotten eggs. Pools of molten iron hiding in the slag
runners, under a thin crust. Take the blade off a shovel
in the blink of an eye; and just as fast, take the foot
right off a leg. Hot winds full of coke dust. Grease and
sweat and man stink beneath the furnace suits. Salt
candy, water by the gallon, bandannas soaked in ice
water, always looking over your shoulder for what might
kill you, always yelling — "fuckin' a" — to be heard
over the roar of huge machines.

Sure, it was hell. But there was dignity, too, in that
work, and the pride of being part of a team, of a hard
and dangerous job done well. And then, at the end of
a long night shift, the furnace ready for the day crew,
and you've got a blessed ten minutes with nothing to
do. Go outside on the steel deck above the slag pits. Try
to catch whatever small breeze comes off the river, and
watch the pale dawn grow until it outshines the fires
of man, outshines the rivers of glowing slag moving
in the pit below and the red and orange fires rising
from the stacks. And it's beautiful. Oh, not beautiful
like sunrise in the mountains, or over the ocean, but
beautiful all the same, even in that hard place. Maybe
it's just your exhaustion, having pushed beyond sleep
four days in a row, but the way the sun comes up big

and orange in the moist air, over the soft green hills,
and the river itself, transformed for a few minutes from
an open sewer to molten silver... There's nothing like it.

****

Nobody makes steel there anymore. Pittsburgh,
Wheeling, Youngstown. Mills all gone or falling down.
Amusement parks, research centers, bike trails and
Home Depots where they used to be. The air and water
are a lot cleaner now. The sky's blue and you can see
the stars at night. There are fish now and fishermen on
the rivers that once carried huge barge trains of coal
and limestone and iron ore on their oily waters. A long
and deep depression has settled deep into the life of the
valley, though. Even Chiodo's is gone.

Maybe it's all for the better. You weigh the clean
air and water, the way the rivers have come back to
life, against the boarded up storefronts, abandoned
downtowns, suicides and divorces, low wage jobs or
no jobs at all.... I don't know. I don't have the heart to
balance the scales of misery and hope and come up with
an answer.

But what I'll always remember of that time is midnight
clouds, half the sky glowing red with the fire of oxygen
blown through a cauldron of steel, white roaring fire
at the heart of a blast furnace, waterfalls of steel
as ladles empty into ingot molds, scream of steel
crushed and flattened in the 5' rollers of the hot rolling
mill. And the dance of soft frail bodies amidst great
machines and fire.

The Valley

The superficial inducements, the exotic, the picturesque
has an effect only on the foreigner. To portray a city, a
native must have other, deeper, motives – motives of one
who travels into the past instead of into the distance.
                                        —Walter Benjamin

1.

I'll take you down to the mill gate on Amity Street
and we'll watch as Davey Havrilla crawls on his hands
and knees, spitting blood and whiskey into the gutter
in front of Ponzi's Bar and Grille on a cold November
night, because Davey never learned to keep his mouth
shut, never learned that there's a time and place, and
this isn't it, and because it's 1970 and he says to no one
in particular but to every steelworker in that bar that
the president is a lying son-of-a-bitch and the war is a
goddamn no-good mess.

And neither his medals and the two fingers he left in
a shit-filled rice paddy outside Da Nang, nor the cold
sweats and nightmares at 2AM can excuse him from the
hard lessons these men feel compelled to stamp into his
flesh with their iron fists.

****

I'll take you to Saint Gregory's Russian Orthodox
church on an April morning, Palm Sunday, where you
will go from the sunlight and new leaves of the maple
trees to the thick dark heat, incense and guttural chants
of the Slavik mass because this is Homestead, 1960 and

this old woman, your mother's mother, has come here
every Sunday and every holy day of obligation of her
long life since she stepped off a train from New York
over 50 years ago, trembling with fear and hope, 16
years old and fleeing her ancestral burden of poverty,
hunger and war. Her fingers, so like the knuckled roots
of a tree that has spent its life slowly shattering rock,
work the black-beaded rosary.

You come not out of piety but a family fealty already
instilled in your 10 year old heart in spite of your
parents' ambivalent desire to wipe the slate clean of the
old world with its old wounds and the ways of their own
parents, instilled through your ancestral peasant DNA.

****

Now it's 1967 and Sharon Lavelle, whom you've known
since her 3rd grade tomboy days when she punched you
in the mouth for telling her that girls couldn't play
third base or any other position for that matter, and
now is about to graduate, drives her older brother's
midnight blue 1964 Mustang along Highway 837, the
only straight stretch of four-lane for miles around, late
May Saturday night, 125 miles per hour, pulling away
now from a primer-gray Camaro as she tops the last
rise, within sight of the Ferris wheel and Thunderbolt
roller coaster at Kennywood Park where your brother
is selling candied apples for $1.60/hour at the end of his
high school sophomore year, and you and your
friends wander amongst the rides, telling mostly lies to
each other about your exploits with girls, lies each of
you wants desperately to believe, as you face down the
long barrel of summer to college or war.

Just then Sharon tops the rise with such speed that her
heart lifts in her chest, the Camaro now well behind her
– she's won! – and as her foot comes off the accelerator,
her right fender clips the guardrail and the car rises,
all of its momentum striving now upward, then sails,
wheels spinning against the sky, Sharon's eyes now
forever fixed on the moon sunk deep in the thick black
waters of the river.

****

Let's go now to the Barnes and Noble that sits where
the Homestead Works once stood, the mill where Frank
Manetti worked for 23 years, where he rolled the steel
girders for the country's bridges and skyscrapers and
30 years later watches the twin towers come down from
the 2-story brick house on Margaret Street where his
parents had died, and he and his wife had raised their
family. He had gone to New York to watch the steel
rise and felt proud enough to tell the man standing
next to him — a complete stranger — of what it was
like to make steel, to be part of the Promethean fires
of industry – Frank the storyteller, Poet of the Rolling
Mill — speaking with an eloquence that delighted
the man, speaking of the great glowing slabs of steel,
the delicate touch of the Heater, his job, the best in
the mill, who had to know just by look and feel the
right time to roll the steel, how this building going up
before their eyes depended upon that knowledge. And
now, right in front of his eyes, it's all coming down, so
terrible, my god, the bodies, the flames, another blow
of the hammer, delivered years after the life he'd known
was shattered in a sovereign collusion of greed and

indifference that brought the valley to its knees, that
wiped out, almost overnight, a way of life, and no one
could believe anything so big, that had endured through
generations, fed so many families, could ever be brought
down so completely.

The phone rings. It's his son, calling from the US Steel
Building a few miles down river where he works. Are
you watching? Jesus, I'm looking out the window here,
50 floors up, trying to imagine. Yes, Frank says, all of
this –waving at the view out the window as if his son
could see, to take in the valley, the river, their lives –
was born in fire. Now look at it.

2.

Do you remember the cinder pots, how the glow from
them played on the bellies of the low clouds, each
pot tipped, in turn, to cast tongues of fire down the
mountain of slag? How your father took you there in
the family's old '49 Plymouth to watch? Our bread and
butter, son. An entire mountain of waste, a mountain
built from the fires that consumed your grandfathers
and in its alchemy created three generations of modest
prosperity but could never consume the body's ancient
desire for green hills and soft black earth.

****

Do you remember your desire to know the headwaters,
the quick, pure mountain streams? In the final year of
high school you pored over maps, traced the branchings
back upstream. In the veins of your bare forearm you

could read the river flowing just under the skin. The first
branching, at McKeesport, where the Youghiogheny
comes in from the east and further south, at Port
Marion, the Cheat flowing out of the mountains of West
Virginia. And the Monongahela itself, never entering
the mountains, but rising from the mine-scarred
hills west of the Appalachians. It was the Cheat that
you picked, tracing it's branchings upstream to the
Blackwater, to Dry Fork, Gandy Creek, deep into the
highlands of West Virginia, and you said this is where I
will live.

****

It's been a good summer and now the bushes sag with
raspberries and huckleberries. She and her two cubs are
strong and fat, they will all survive the winter. She has
known this high meadow all of her 10 years and never
have the berries been so good. A small creek flows
from the dark mouth of a cave, the first of the gathering
waters, here in the pine forests of West Virginia, high
on Spruce Mountain, and the air is cool and smells of
earth and water and a dank musk rising from the cave.
It reminds her of the winter's den. There is no other
world for her. The cubs, sated, wrestle in the grass, then
fall asleep. She pauses for a moment to check on them,
shits on the bank of the creek, and goes back to eating.

Michael Adams

Headwaters

Begins the river from dark forest
of hemlock and pine, from this
long-backed mountain, springs
from moist, green earth as rivulet,
and as it falls, grows to creek,
through pasture, through canyons to pass
its youth in wild exuberance
before it spends itself upon the plains,
bent to the unyielding thrust
of industry, shackled
to the pauper spirit of our times.

Begins the river on Allegheny upland,
this deep-cut plateau of wind and sky,
begins this beast of man's narrow greed,

Here yet unburdened and ever new.

I Went Out

"I have met with but one or two persons in the course of my
life who understood the art of Walking."
                                    —*H.D. Thoreau*

I went out to the woods, the wild rolling rocky woods
and folded ancient hills of West Virginia,

Whistled and wandered, rambled with Thoreau,
scrambled on the crags with Snyder, wrestled with Heidegger
on rainy nights with whiskey and black coffee.

Sought truth with a young man's single-minded
passion, sought god in rock and tree,
cloud and storm, creek and mountain laurel,
woman's smile and sway of hip.

Young and willful in the old, old hills,
folded round and rocky, hemlock, oak and maple,
dogwood blossom Appalachian hills.
With friends, with lovers, or alone, but always
with the woods,
happy, broken-hearted
or not knowing which,
wandering the wild rugged hills.

What We Ate

I'll tell you what we ate that winter.
It was cold on that mountain.
And my God, the snow!
Started late, just
before Christmas, but didn't quit
until two weeks after Groundhog's Day.

Duane shot the sow a week before Thanksgiving
with a .22 in the middle of her forehead.

We hoisted her on the engine hoist,
slit her open from throat to groin.
The entrails steamed
in the hard air.

The dogs went crazy, of course,
when Kate threw them
the guts and she had
to knock Big Red Dog
near senseless
with a cast-iron skillet
to keep him from killing Bull Lee.

We used long knives like razors and were covered
to our elbows in blood and fat.
Moon Woman scraped the hide clean
and salted it for tanning.

Big pots of boiling water,
slow fire in the smokehouse.
Big Red Dog, back
on his feet, fighting,
with Bull Lee over the head.

All winter —
bacon and chops
loins and roasts
potatoes and turnips.
Spinach drizzled in pork fat.
We ate like kings. We cut and split 10 cords
of firewood – oak, maple, black locust. Everything
came from that mountain.

It was beautiful up there,
I wouldn't have traded it
for anything in the world,
but that soil never
gave up anything
without a fight.

That night, Moon Woman in the sauna, her breasts
long and thin, nipples big, almost black.
Her snatch, dark,
beaded with sweat.

Outside, hot from the sauna,
she pushed me down
into the straw,
said – I'm hungry –
as she rode me.

What we'd done that day –
I'd never done anything like it.
I was in love with all of it.

The stars spread their arms
over us. Pale Moon Woman
moaning, steam rising from her knobbed back
like mist from a forest after rain.

The molten core of us exploding,
life and death, shape-shifting, one
into the other and the other
again. No man no woman
one being, the warm animal of ourselves
so greedy, so hungry to take it all in,
give it all away.

Moon Woman, her long hair gleaming starlight,
sways over as we ride, cradled
upon the star-domed earth.

Work

I drive the winding two-lane that falls from the eastern
flank of the Allegheny Mountains, along Seneca Creek
to the valley of the Potomac, then south toward the
headwaters, broad green fields beneath towering ridges,
the small towns of Seneca Rocks, Riverton, Circleville,
Cherry Grove. Then back up out of the valley, the dirt
track leading upward, through the long slanting gold
of a June evening to my small cabin high on Spruce
Mountain. The next day I help Wayne — he and Carol
my nearest neighbors— a mile further up the mountain,
take down a 50' post oak, lightning-struck two years
ago, dead and now threatening their barn. It falls
clean between two white oaks – Wayne's skill with a
chainsaw, a lifetime in the woods – and we buck it into
firewood. All day, cutting wood in the mountains I
love, and loving the work but thinking of money, money
I don't have, money I need. At dinner that evening,
exhausted, two cords bucked, split with the hydraulic
splitter, Carol's venison stew, but I'm thinking of work
and money. That night, alone in my cabin, I read the
poems of Han Shan, wanting to slip the bounds of this
earth and fly with him amidst the clouds. But I cannot.

> Longing to remain in the hills
> I must return to the city,
> look for work.

****

Splitting wood all morning
black locust hard as iron, the maul
rings through the valley, beneath this ring

of mountains, 30 dollars
for a day's work, and I'm strung
on a wire between mountains and city.

Here at the headwaters, the spring
outside the cabin door cold and pure.

But no work.

Zen and poetry are no help.

Enough cash to gas the car,
buy a few groceries.

****

First snow of the autumn dusts the ridge tops.
Lift the maul and inhale
swing from the heels
aim beyond what you want to hit
the hills ring as the maul
strikes the wedge
and the round splits clean and true,
light purple veining
through the white wood.

Next week
or the week after –
back to the city,
to look for work.

Michael Adams

This Isn't What You're Paid For

If you hadn't seen this a thousand times
already, you might give a damn.

600 feet straight down to the cobblestones

    if you fell from here you'd have time to think about it alright!

the blocky masses
of the old courthouse and jail,
the two rivers –
one slate blue, the other
green-brown, mixing
to form the big Ohio,
the steep green of Mount Washington

And the sky
    the smoke blown clean to New Jersey by the cold front
    deep blue with an enormous storm brewing in the north.

Like I said, it's quite a view out that window, but you're not
being paid to look out windows, no they're paying you
$3.27 an hour to wash them.

And all these rows and rows of cheap suits hunched over desks
aren't being paid to gaze out windows either.
Whatever it is they're so busy doing, through the ringing
of phones and the clatter of typewriters,
it's important enough for somebody with plenty
of money to pay them to do it, and believe me,
it's not looking out windows.

Do that on your own time, unless
you're one of those men in Armani suits
in the corner offices where you have to be extra careful

not to get even a drop of water on the desk or rug
or it might just cost you your job.
They can look out windows all they want,
in their mirror-shiny Italian shoes on the deep
pile rugs, standing behind the empty gleaming desks,
backs turned, standing at the big windows,
talking on the speaker phones.
Those men can look out windows all they want, as long
as they deliver the goods – bring the crude up
from the deep waters of the Gulf, get McKeesport
to turn out more steel pipe
without overtime, squeeze a little blood
out of everyone not being paid
to gaze out windows.

It's their empire out those windows,
built on the blood and sweat of millions just like you,
the men and women who did the real work.

You gotta squeeze, that's they're motto.

And believe me, they better not catch you
looking out windows.

Michael Adams

Do You See That Woman?

Do you see that woman there? In front of the bookstore.
She's coming from work, one job to the next,
10:05 in the morning, waiting for a bus.
You don't recognize her? Sure you do,
look more closely. That's right,
she works in the cafeteria, starts at 5:00,
serves you toast and scrambled eggs.
A couple of your friends were in high spirits the other day,
joking about the food, called the eggs sawdust.
Right in front of her. You could have said something.
Sawdust –
How do you think that made her feel?

Okay, you're young, and you've never
had to face it, how it wears you down, the small
daily humiliations that come at you from all directions,
but here's something you should know. Everybody
wants to take pride in their work.
Learn that one thing, really learn it,
and you'll do okay in life.

Look at her. A small woman, almost tiny, skin
as brown as the earth, hair jet black, streaked with white.
It's raining, she's standing under the awning, reading a book.
See how soft everything looks through the rain —
      her face, the sky, the tan stone buildings and the green hills.

It might surprise you to know that she once played cello in a
      string quartet
in the capital of her native land. But that was before the war,
      before it all went so wrong.
She doesn't need anything from you; she's got her life
and if it's not everything she dreamed it would be, well, whose is?

You should go up to her and say hello. It wouldn't hurt,
a small thing that might make her day. But you won't,
it would never cross your mind – not out of meanness, no,
nothing like that – but because you think
the world was made all new for you,
because you don't understand yet that the life
you're waiting so eagerly for will come to you bent,
hobbling on crutches. You still think
it will fly to you on wings.

Jimmy's Song

Jimmy's thinkin' of you as he rattles his bones on the way home
love bones, love bones, snake-eyes in the hand.

Holey old rusty Rambler rattles along under the gray
smokestack sky, over the cobblestone streets, windows wide
to the hot city grime, weavin' the diesel fume
dreams of semis & buses, sweat stains, grit of the day
ground under the skin,
dirty old city skin.
& the groan & roll, hum & moan
of Jimmy's punch the clock, bitch & brawl world,
work your life away for the man world,
all ground under the skin, ground in, & it ain't never
comin' out.

But it's 3:00 on Friday afternoon & Jimmy don't give
a fuck, he's gonna forget it all for a couple of days,
gonna shake those yellowed ivory bones,
fast-talkin', sharp-dressin' card-shark bones,
Sisters of the Sacred Heart Mission bones,
in the hot wind & the gritty sky,
cruisin' the ether looking for song.
It's Otis & his horns to send him home —
Shake! & his backbone slips,
& Jimmy's poor old beat bone rises.
Shake in the hot gray afternoon, across the greasy gray river.

Hum of tires on the steel deck,
light & shadows through the girders of the Stanwix Street Bridge,
Rambler, take those tired old love bones over that big river,
take those love bones home.

Two hundred windows,
50 floors up,

every damn one of them sparkling,
Jimmy & his bucket and bright blue overalls,
& the rows and rows of office bees –
blue-collar blues & white collar moan,
& the rich bastards in their rich bastard offices,
& the Man just getting' richer as everybody else
goes down.

But it's Friday afternoon & Jimmy's bouncing along the cobblestones
as the old yellow bones rattle from the rearview,
thousand dollar bones, the biggest score
Jimmy ever made —
lucky seven, lucky Jimmy,
but that was years ago, before
the punch the clock days,
diaper and bottle,
never a good nights sleep days,
but hey, it's okay.

Jimmy's got money in his pocket, a woman to spend it
& he's ready for love,
& he's thinkin' of you in the shower,
washin' away the dirt of your day,
the stink of the hospital,
bedpans & vomit,
dirty water down the drain,
waiting for his love bones.
Clean & eager –

Loves bones, love bones, snake-eyes in the hand.
Baby, call your mother to watch the kid,
put some Rocks on ice, Jimmy'll fire up the grill,
rib-eyes & corn, you're gonna party tonight.
Water beads & back, breasts & ass –
love bones, love bones —
long strong thighs

Otis shakes him up onto Arlington, Wicked Pickett takes him up the hill
to Knoxville. Jimmy, poppin' his fingers & singing sweet harmony
& now he's stalled out in rush hour
but Brother Pickett's got him groovin' in the Midnight Hour,
through the horns, hot drivers and changin' of the lights,
& three black girls in a Camaro next to him say,
turn it up and they groove together 'till the light
turns green & Jimmy's hot & ready, baby, money in his pocket,
Friday night, fired up & sweaty,
thinkin' of you, thinkin' of the fast moving women
all day down below his shiny windows,
the long-legged ones, busy & bright,
high heels clicking, someplace to go
& Jimmy's up there looking down on it all.
McKinley Park & he's almost home,
Aretha, take him home.
People Get Ready, there's a train a comin'.
Love bones love bones —
baby, get ready,
fuckin' or fightin' tonight
& you decide.
Jimmy'll take the first any day.
A roll of the dice
here comes Jimmy.
There's a train a comin' —
comin' home to you.

Sweet

All is Well!—This was what Charlie Parker/Said when he played, All is Well.

—*Jack Kerouac*

Horns & whiskey
& the light graying into dawn,
with Bird or Billie, or Ornette
on the turntable, the only thing
in that shitty basement apartment
worth a damn.
Only two or three of us left by then,
so late, the hardcore, the sleepless,
fueled by that inexhaustible
need to grab it all, whatever
it was, as much as we could,
knowing all the while
we could never get enough.

God, how we would talk, argue,
fight for hours — jazz, the Beats,
the blues & rock & roll,
Nixon, Kissinger, the war & all
the goddamn liars.

There was booze & weed,
plenty of it, but none of us
burned as hot as you —
the white crosses
so your body could soar
as high as your heart
& the Qualudes to drag you,
finally, into dreamless sleep.
Cockroaches & coke in the sugar bowl,
none of us were saints, but you,

you thought nothing could touch you.

& by God, for a while nothing could,
holy & shining, the way
you had with women, & that horn
raw & sweet at the same time, so much
beauty & pain at once, shards of buried glass
& the pure sands of a wave-washed beach.

You came back but could never come home
from the green hell of Vietnam with a craving
nothing could fill for long & such a love
like I've never seen for every
breeze & tear & sunrise.
Oh you could blow, I mean
that horn & you said you wanted to blow
the whole damned laughing, crying,
loving, dying, fighting world
through that horn, breathe it all in
& turn everything that was ugly holy.

Like that night-turning-to-morning
you said, let's go & we went up
into the city & the sun
came up orange & cold & you
wet your lips & launched
into Bird — After You've Gone,
while the bridges filled with cars
& the sun burned off the frost & then
you slowed it way down with I Can't Get

Started, but what it was was you couldn't
stop & nobody could follow where you went
& none of us could accept what you needed
to give & finally we stopped trying.
It wasn't just me, I wasn't the only

one who cut you to the bone, but when you finally
fled Pittsburgh for Denver
on that 3 AM Greyhound nobody
was happy but we all
breathed a sigh of relief.

You sent a couple of letters at first,
boasting about all the girls, how bright
the stars were, the huge heart of the night,
a different address every month or so,
& I sent a few postcards to whatever
address I had, with not much to report on,
& soon enough I stopped or you,
I don't remember.

We all settled into the routines we once said never to,
but I'd think of you sometimes, knowing you
could never settle into anything like a routine
& years later I heard from somebody who heard
from somebody that there was a bum
they found frozen one January morning,
an old vet from Pittsburgh they thought,
with nothing to his name but a bedroll & an alto sax,
who haunted Colfax Ave.
& oh,
but could he blow sweet.

Michael Adams

God's Son Lay Down

God's son walked down the street, His son
walked down East Colfax Ave. on a Jan. morning,
1AM, in the snow, torn
sneakers and an alto sax and nowhere
to rest his head, nowhere except
in the lap of an old junkie whore,
and God's son lay down his dark head there,

Lay down his head on the altar of flesh
weary of preaching love,
offering his music of love.
But no one hears –
that we are all each other,
and all one, and each
of us is holy
and the earth is holy,
this old battered boot-worn earth.

But no one hears and so God's son
lay down his head again to die
and be reborn with the new day, reborn to preach
his only commandment,

To love that old bum, that old drunk vet,
that old woman smelling of vomit
and despair who once was
someone's daughter,
and someone's daughter on the street now –
15 years old and run-away, pregnant punching bag
with needle nightmares,

His son lay down his head because no one
wanted to hear about love, only
about vengeance and sin,

And God's son lay down his weary head
with it's undying burden of sorrow,
which is no more or less than joy offered
and not taken, lay down
his weary head in a back alley in the snow
in the lap of an old whore
and blew softly, softly
to his Father, the prayer
of his music.

Michael Adams

Trains Like the River

The steel wheels were always rolling,
up and down the valley, loaded with coal and grain,
trucks and ore and gut-searing chlorine
and sulfur in the black tanker cars.

They rolled through Homestead,
South Side, over in the Strip District
with frozen sides of beef and big boxes
of Lake Erie smelts.

They rolled across Lysle Boulevard in McKeesport
while rush hour commuters cooked in their own idling exhaust,
rolled through high school summer nights,
with Bob Prince – the Gunner –
announcing the Pirate games while I sat
on the back porch with a lemonade,
listening to Woody Fryman's almost-perfect
game against the Mets – July 1, 1966, a lead-off single
to Ron Hunt then 27 batters down in a row.

You could hear the long whistle
of the McKesport Connecting Railroad locomotive
leaving Duquesne with a train of slag pots bound
for the big dump out by the county airport.

Down in Panther Hollow, graduate school days,
and the tracks just across Boundary Street,
where Harvey
          — son of Holocaust survivors, lover of jazz and
Kerouac —
now a doctor in Sacramento –
taught me how to hop a freight
so if you slipped you'd fall away
and not under the wheels.

Trains like the river,
always rolling on, bound for places
I'd never been but I learned the roads

      Denver & Rio Grande   Burlington Northern
              Pennsylvania & Lake Erie
      Acheson, Topeka & Santa Fe

and rolled the names of the towns
around on my tongue

      Bangor, Maine   Cheyenne, Wyoming
          Denver   Kankakee   Topeka
      Biloxi   New Orleans

late at night, haunted by the lonely whistle
calling me to the road

Wobbly Joe

My friend Harvey wrote me the other day about a memory that
came to him while he was bicycling, came out of nowhere, of
a January night in Pittsburgh many years ago, when he and I
were at a bar on the Southside to hear a bluegrass band. What
came so vividly was "lingering on the sidewalk, 1 or 2AM, pure
crystalline frost in the dry cold air, and pissing off the curb
because it seemed the thing to do." I don't know if I remember
that particular night— there were so many nights of music
and bars back then. Maybe I've constructed a composite from
several of them, but this is what comes to mind — A local band
with guitar, fiddle, banjo and bass and they were damn good,
a little rough around the edges but they had a lot of energy and
the music went straight to the gut — Southern Appalachian
tunes, murder and hard times. The bar was Wobbly Joe's, a
place that drew mill workers, students, and radicals, something
you don't see anymore in these days of globalization and
outsourcing. It was across Carson Street from the Southside
Works of J&L Steel. I kept my Wobbly Joe's t-shirt years
beyond serviceable life, a rag full of holes with the great
IWW songwriter Joe Hill, as big as King Kong, right arm
raised, palm open in greeting, striding over a factory. I loved
Pittsburgh in those days, the cold dirty streets, the hills and
rivers, fire and stink of the mills, the gritty river towns, and
at the same time I couldn't wait to leave, there was something
in me, an itch to get out, move on, it didn't matter where, just
pick a direction and go. It was the late 70s, I was fresh out
of grad school and everybody was leaving, Pittsburgh was the
end of the line, a 3AM bus station when your money's run out,
a dinner of scalded coffee and Saltine's with ketchup, the last
town on the mid-west bowling circuit. The whole battered old
dying industrial world was right there on Carson Street, and
in those sunless narrow valleys and the mill towns clinging to
the hillsides, with the heart of the continent open and calling
to the west. Harvey was in his last year of medical school and

in a few years he would be in Sacramento and I would be in
Colorado. We'd had four or five pitchers of Rolling Rock
and walked over to the railroad tracks to clear our heads.
There was a string of empty ore cars, two locomotives idling,
and we tossed pebbles into the last car just to hear the deep
hollow clang. After a few minutes the pitch of the locomotives
changed, a long groan came down the train and there was the
rapid hammering of steel on steel as the slack came out of the
cars and the couplings came taut. The train started to move,
slow, and we walked along with it, the river black and shining,
a red glow rising from the furnaces on the other side, over in
Hazelwood. The train was moving faster now and I felt the
whole great bulk of the earth begin to slide away under my feet
as I ran to keep up, slide away, the earth turning towards the
distant dawn, the whole city moving beneath me, the rivers and
green hills falling away to prairie, the night settling, and me
running west under the bright winter stars.

Letters

New York City   **Jan. 1982**

Dear Mike,

I don't know how long it's been since I meant to write
this letter. Longer ago than spring I guess. What's
spring like out there? Seasons lose their force in a
city like this. The lighted temperature signs change
numbers, people change their clothes – and fashions –
and that's about it.

I'm working for this moving company now – trucks
with bad brakes, bad shocks, scrapes all over, driven by
underpaid and overworked madmen. This is my second
day in a row off and I'm STILL beat. Years are like
greased pigs and I guess what I need is a net.

Anyway how about some news of my trip, careening
across America, searching for wisdom and sex. By
3AM of the day after I left Boulder I found myself
outside of Omaha. There was an easiness to the whole
thing, but then, no rides. I was cold, real shivering
cold. I began to curse the cars. By the next evening I
was outside Davenport, Iowa and just beat, beat down
and used up. I bailed out, did what had to be done, and
walked the miles into town and got a bus. I saw early
morning Chicago and then what Harvey called the
bowling circuit: Cleveland, Toledo, etc.

I did meet some interesting people. There was a
farming couple from Iowa – late middle-age. They had
never seen New York and that didn't seem to strike
them as a crucial failure of their lives. I guess this great

rotting epitaph is not the center of the universe after all.

Harvey said something about going out your way last time we spoke. We could have a reunion and climb a bottle of Jack Daniels .

Michael

Homeville, PA   **June 1982**

Dear Son,

Glad to know all is well with you. Your mother and I really enjoyed your call last Sunday. I've finally got my muscles working again, so I'm busy getting the yard in shape, but I do tire rather easily. This getting old is for the birds.

The weather is as nuts as the economy. The skies are as blue around here now as they are in Boulder since the mills shut down. J& L is down completely on the South Side. Homestead has shut down OH #5 and the only blast furnace in the whole valley is at Edgar Thompson Works in Braddock. Clairton's down completely and so is Duquesne. If it weren't for unemployment compensation and pensions this would be as bad as back in the 30s. You should be glad you got away from here.

I guess change is inevitable. We old folks talk about the good old days, but that's a crock. The only thing good about them was we were young and that's what we miss.

Well, son. Take care and God bless.

Love
Dad

Pittsburgh   **May 1983**

Dear Michael,

Thank you for your very nice letter to me after your last
visit here. I know you were very preoccupied with your
father's funeral. I hope things have settled and that you
are able to go on with a subdued sadness.

Have you seen Dick? Tell him I said hello. I ran into
Sue Ross at the demonstration against Reagan. Did
you know she is separated? She wishes you well.

I've been working an awful lot but maybe things will
slow down for the summer. I'll try working full time
when school starts; I sure like having my own money,
but I'll probably have to cut back.

Take care, write and call me.
Love you,
Maria

Homeville, PA   **August 1983**

Dear Michael,

Jeanne called me this morning from Oklahoma. She
drove the 15 hour trip all alone. I didn't tell her that
it scares me to death knowing she's driving alone and
sleeping at truck stops. She is very cocky and sure of
herself. I could sure use some of that.

I'm sorry I never answered your girlfriend's letter and
now that you two are no longer together it doesn't seem
to make much sense. Maybe it's just as well, because I

didn't know what I was doing or saying back them. I missed him so much. I still do. One thing I do know – I really appreciated her thoughtfulness. I better close for now. Think of your old mom back here.

God Bless You,
Mom

Sacramento   **Dec. 1984**

Dear Mike,

Today is my post-call day off. Somehow I enjoy weekends off more than weekdays. I get more things done, like writing letters to some of my favorite characters.

I've been dating one of our new general surgeons at work, a wonderful woman with the unlikely name of Scarlet LaRue. We have a lot in common and she has a real surgical mentality – bold and self-disciplined, never loses her cool.

I got a letter and a phone call from, of all people, Diana! She's come to enjoy Pittsburgh and will be there another full year. I can tell you I still have a warm spot for her. I think you should look her up when you visit Steeler country. She always liked you.

Love,
Harvey

Wet Mountains   **Jan. 2003**

Dear Dad,

Well, it's been a long time since I've written. But I
woke up – it's the middle of the night but my bladder
won't let me get a full night's sleep anymore – and I was
thinking about you. It's been 20 years almost to the day
since you died, and I didn't even think about that but I
woke up with you on my mind, so I guess it was floating
around in there.

It's 12 below zero and the wind's blowing pretty good,
but it's warm in the cabin with a fire going. You'd like
it here. The stars are so close, up here at 9,000 feet. I
think you'd be proud of me, building this cabin with my
own two hands, just like you did our first house back
there on Elizabeth St.

The world's changed so much – I've changed so much –
that I don't know where to start.   First off, I'm married
and pretty happy — been together over ten years now!
No kids, though. I don't know why, just one of those
things. I always had something else going on and by the
time I stopped and looked back it was just too late.

Mom's doing well. Almost 82; never remarried, said no
one could ever replace you. You know, it was awfully
hard on her, the way you went, so sudden. Hard on all
of us. Till then that's how I thought I wanted to go, but
now I think it's better to die slowly. Gives your loved
ones time for good-byes.

Looks like we're heading into another war. This
president seems hell bent on it and I think it's going to
be a real mess, just like Vietnam. You talked me out

of that one. Remember that night toward the end of my senior year in high school? I wanted to join the Marines. We talked for a long time, out on the back porch, a light rain doing a *rat-tat-tat* on the awning. You told me that it was a terrible war, that nobody knew why we were there or how we'd get out or what all the death and killings were for. You wouldn't talk about the terrible winter you spend in the Ardennes Forest in 1945, but you made it clear that this war wasn't worth the life of your son.

I never thanked you for that. It wasn't too long after that we weren't talking much at all. I took my passion for changing the world in a different direction. Now I think you were sympathetic, but believed I knew too little, wanted to go too far, too fast. We were all, young and old, caught up in the roller coaster ride of the 60s and all any of us could do was hang on.

I'm glad for nights like this, when I wake up and can't get back to sleep. A near-full moon shining on the snow, the wind in the trees. You'd like this land – a high, rolling country of sage and pines. You talked often of Colorado, of how you fell in love with it in your Army days.

You know, it reminds me of Homeville, and of my farm in West Virginia. You can't see the high mountains from here, just rolling tree covered hills and deep valleys. I think that's why I chose it. Funny, isn't it? A guy moves halfway across the country to get away and then picks a place that reminds him of home.

Well, dad, that's about it for now.

Love,
Michael

Ghosts

Stand on the bluffs above the old river late on a
winter's afternoon. A low, gray sky hides the setting
sun. Strain to see through the falling snow the ancient
rusting furnaces, the cathedrals of industry, that strove
for heaven and though failing, fell not as far short as
you might think.

Be very quiet and you might hear the cries of men and
women whose hearts and bodies have been scarred and
hardened far beyond the years they carry. Look hard
for them, reaching out to touch rivers of molten steel, to
be consumed by poverty and the greed of the mighty.

They speak in old languages from an old world if
they are our grandfathers or great-grandfathers or
they speak as we speak if they are our fathers or our
fathers' sons, in the aggressive and optimistic tongue of
America. Whatever languages they speak, listen for
the sorrow of a way of life that once seemed as enduring
as the river, now gone for good. It was a hard life that
broke men and broke women, yet it was a life that
promised something better and, through years of sweat
and struggle, strikes and beatings, delivered on that
promise, if not for them at least for their children and
grandchildren.

Stay a little longer even though it grows dark and you
are chilled to the bone, and you will hear the hopeful
voices of young women, bent to the hard labors of the
sweat shops and laundries, and the small birds of their
dreams, and the hard-faced men talking in unions halls,
the Sokol Halls, the bars of Braddock, Homestead,
Duquesne, McKeesport. You might also hear the
echoes of strikers from another century, the sound of

machine guns and the steel-shod hooves of horses as mounted troopers ride down cobbled streets.

What you hear and almost see are only ghosts. What you will see when the sun rises are the long and empty expanses of weeds and ruin where once a nation and people were forged in sweat and pain, and the dying hopeless towns of old men and old women, soot-blackened brick and boarded storefronts.

And through it all, the river — opaque, powerful, uncaring. It's flow, it's course, is the course of your life, wherever you go, scribed to its sea-reaching waters.

Swallows

I got Cathy's letter today and walked around the house
for a good long time, crumpled it up, threw it away,
picked it up and smoothed it out. Then I got a beer,
went out to the back fence, sat on a downed cottonwood
along the creek and drank to you beneath the stars.
Well, damn, brother, damn, just goddamn.

Remember that night a week or so before I left for
Colorado and we drank until we closed that bar on
Bates St. (what was the name of it?) and then walked
to where we could look down on the river and the Hot
Metal bridge and the mill and they tapped the furnace
and you recited Milton while we watched the red glow?
            with hideous ruin and combustion down
            To bottomless perdition there to dwell
            in Adamantine Chains and penal Fire

And I said, that's what a Master's degree in English
gets you, Milton and steady work in the rolling mill and
you laughed and said, there are birds that live there,
generations after generation, the mill and the river, its
their world and all they know. We were both quite for a
minute or so, and then you said, just wait, you're going
to miss all of this.

I can see between the spare lines of her letter how it
went down, 8 years in the rolling mill, then the lay-
offs and the days that stretched to weeks and then
months, the part-time jobs while you pretended to
yourself that the mills would start up again one day.
You'd walk down to the river each afternoon with a
cooler of Rolling Rock, beneath the yellow span of the
Birmingham bridge, down to the broken pier where we
used to fish and drink and never caught anything but

carp, sharp-teethed and evil smelling. You said you
were writing a novel about the mills, the decline of steel
– a big-hearted rusting ruin of a book, you called it.
When anyone asked you how the writing was going you
just needed time, time for it to stew and ferment. Then
finally Cathy said, can't you see it's over? How many
chances did she give you? And you added a bottle of
whiskey to the beer and , if you remembered, a cold cod
sandwich wrapped in greasy wax paper.

Yeah, I can see it, that last day, when they started to
tear the mill down and you set your line in the water,
raised a beer to salute the last of the day, the calm slate
waters of the river, the furnaces where the red iron
would never run again.

Damn you. What right did you have? The rest of us
could fall in the mud, curse somebody, anybody —
the steel companies, the government, god, fate, pick
ourselves up and limp on. A lot of people said good
riddance when they tore the mills down. But not you,
no, you believed there were promises that had to be
kept. Such a romantic. You were in love with rust and
ruin. Did you think anybody owed you anything?

It must have seemed so right and inevitable in the end,
no matter the mess you left behind. I hope that at the
last the setting sun broke from beneath the clouds to
bathe the wild tangle of your red hair, the river, the
unglassed windows of the empty mill in its soft light. In
the end I hope it released a flight of swallows.

Homestead Blues

Joe Magarac and John Henry are down on Seventh
Avenue, past the end of Amity Street, playing for tips
where the rolling mill used to be. Yeah it's a shindig
in steeltown, with Joe on the lap steel and John Henry
on guitar and harp. You gotta make ends meet when
you're on the street and they've got one hell of a
repertoire — Muddy Waters, Mississippi John Hurt,
Robert Johnson and low down growlin' Howlin' Wolf.
They've lived the blues, man, and they know how to
play 'em. You can't swing that double-jack or bend
them red hot bars forever, those days are long gone and
it's time to get up and get on, so drop a dollar or two,
whatever you can spare, in that open guitar case, 'cause
they're pouring their hearts and souls into it, singing
about something gone and it ain't never coming back,
you know it brother, but sister as long as we got it in
song we got it in our hearts and it won't ever die.

Maybe you'll wander down there late at night when
the clouds are blowing fast across a moonless sky,
down past the long rusting buildings, broken glass,
through the weeds, and there's nobody else around but
if you're quiet and lucky you might hear voices down
by the old pumphouse. Maybe it's Joe and John and
maybe Woody, too and Joe Hill, Cisco and Sonny and
Leadbelly, all of them down on the riverbank, jammin'
away, singing the sweet, low sad songs, singing about
getting knocked down and dragging yourself back up,
time after time, but you do it, you keep doing it and
that's what counts, makes you a man or a woman.
That's when you wanna sit down, just sit down and be
quiet and let that music and that longing and the old,
old river carry you away.

Where We Come From

The House on Lincoln Ave.

I have to go into this house now, where a woman and man
fought to raise their children out of poverty.
I have to lift the sagging roof, hold back the ravages
of time and neglect, square the door frames.
I must lift this neighborhood from its decline,
back into the world of sin and laughter.

Where are the young mothers who fretted with each other
over coffee, hung laundry with an eye, always,
for their wayward sons, cooked potatoes and pork roasts
and practiced patience with their men, when they spent their
        paychecks
at Wasko's Bar and Grill or laid bets with the bagman down
        on Sixth Ave.?

I have to walk into the gloom of that bar and take my father
by the arm and tell him – the War
made you distant, but that's over now.
It's time to come home.

Andrew

My father had grown up fatherless, crisscrossed the country
during the Great Depression and was happiest when moving.
He loved to walk and so that is what he did for a living –
a wounded man walking the neighborhoods of Pittsburgh,
knocking on doors, talking to housewives, old vets from an
        earlier war,
steelworkers mowing the lawn before the afternoon shift.
Writing the vital facts of their lives on pink index cards.

He would take me for walks around the neighborhood
Saturday mornings, talking about old Mr. & Mrs. Lawlor,
how they lost a son in Korea, or the strange but gentle Munz's
who had fled German in 1939
because of their Quaker beliefs.

I loved the man but feared him.
There was dark violence, deeply hidden
that sometimes bubbled to the surface –
the angry words, the belt whipped
from the belt loops of his trousers,
the coiled whip of the man himself, looming
over me, and then, just as quickly, the mumbled curse,
the shake of his head two or three times,
the turning away.

First Love

In the spring of 1958 I would walk Wren home from school.
Nine years old and we were in love.
One rainy April afternoon, under the black dome of the
        umbrella together,
I pointed up and said, it's like the night sky, when it's cloudy
and there are no stars, and she hugged me
and kissed me right on the lips.
That spring we talked about the stars, I told her of rockets
that would one day take us to the moon and beyond.
She took me to her family's flower garden, rich
with the smell of roses and she told me that when we grew up
she would grow a hundred different kinds of roses and when I
came home from work the smell of roses would fill the house.

That summer while I was away at camp,
her family moved away and I never saw her again.

Adventure

We boys had free rein to explore the town
and by the time I was eight Bobby Evans, Jackie Gueron
and I had discovered the woods just beyond the town hall.
We'd cross the small greasy creek that flowed along Homeville
      Rd.,
ignoring the rusted face-shot signs that warned us
in bold red and black lettering
              DANGER! AREA CLOSED! STAY OUT!
 and head to the barren hills where only weeds and twisted
      shrubs grew
and the smoke and gas of the underground
coal mine fires rose through fissures where the coal pillars
had burned away and collapsed the earth.
We pretended we had found the Lost World
and imagined dinosaurs and head hunters.

What a world we lived in!
So broken and damaged, yet so new to us –
we knew nothing else—
so big and full of adventure.

Terezia

She sat cross-legged on her apartment floor, wearing cut-off
      jeans.
Her name was Terezia and she had been born in Hungary.
One of her earliest memories was of tanks in the streets, the
      glasses
on the dining room table dancing as they passed, an explosion,
a burning tank, a young man running, hands thrust to heaven,
his head on fire.

The first time she took me to bed, she held my penis
and placed my hand between her legs.
Wait, she said, maybe tomorrow, and the next night
we made love and she yelled NO! NO! with an urgency
that belied the words and yet I pulled back but not out and
       stopped,
husbanding within that small kernel of cruelty that lies
at the heart of all teasing until she said Come On! and then
       I did
and she did and said NO! again and then OH! and I was lost,
       tumbling
into the rolling curves of her, falling into her dark eyes.

The next morning, over coffee, I was quiet in the long golden
October light, wondering what it might mean for us to tangle
no and yes in the same hot froth of passion.

The Fires Go Cold

Monessen, 1983.
I have to go to this mill town south of Pittsburgh
on a Monday morning in November where the fires of the iron
       furnaces
have gone cold and the reek of dead fish rises
from the vaults of the Mellon Bank, and walk into the bars,
up to the houses and tell the men and women there, yes,
what was done to you here stinks far worse
than dead fish but your protests are no use, your jobs
are never coming back.
The men who have decided your fate have never been to your
       town and never will be.
They don't know work, they only know money.
And I have to let them crucify me for bringing this news,

for breaking faith and walking away, leaving them to huddle
around the cold fires of their lives.

****

The echoes fade, but never die.
I wake in the middle of the night,
half a continent, half a century removed.
A woman lies next to me, breathing softly,
infinitely far away. I could reach out.
There would be solace, comfort
in the long warmth of her.

Outside a storm plays itself out,
flashes of lightning and the roll
of thunder, farther and farther way.

Joseph Mikula

I'm wandering through Saint Michael's Cemetery in
Homeville, PA. My father's buried here, my grandparents,
and we'll lay our mother to rest here when her time comes.
It's a nice place – well-kept, green and wooded. It's a
beautiful spring day, the sky blue and not a cloud. I put
new flowers on the graves, then walk around the grounds.
These were people I knew as a child – tough and strong.
Working-class Poles, Slovaks, Ukrainians. The men worked
in the mills and factories, the women stayed home to raise
the kids and hold the household together.

Here's Joseph Mikula – 1910-1966. I remember you, Joe.
One day you were walking around, gruff and loud, a real
joker. Getting ready for a fishing trip in a few days up to
Pymatuming Reservoir. Then ... boom, on the ground,
heaving like a hooked fish on land, eyes bugged out, skin
blue-gray, dead before they got you to the hospital. You
were looking forward to that trip – a little fishing, a lot of
beer and booze with the boys. You were a lot more fun
than my own parents. I'd come by Saturday mornings
with the paper and you'd be under the hood of one car
or another, take the paper from me, hands covered with
grease. How about a beer, you'd say? How old are you
now? Sixteen, huh? Old enough for pussy, old enough for
beer. I'd just turn red and look down at my feet.

I hear you stirring around down there. Forty years gone
and it still doesn't sit well with you. You were so full of
life And you too, Mary – 1913-1996 — beloved wife and
mother. They could have added long-suffering. It was no
secret he drank too much, though he was a happy drunk,
even the time he wrapped the car around the light pole up
the street. Mary, you lived a long life and all you want now
is to rest, but he won't let you. Always on you, wasn't he?

Mary, wherz ma goddamm boots? Mary, wherz ma lunch,
I'm late fa work, fa christsakes.

Five days a week, the same thing — You hand him his
black steel lunch box; the screen door bangs as he heads
out to his '62 Chevy Impala and the 4 to 12 shift at O.H.
5. Roast beef and American cheese on Jewish rye, a Vlasic
pickle, an apple and two Snickers bars. Every day for
30 years. He grabs a coffee and glazed donut in the mill
cafeteria before the daily meeting for the afternoon crew
and reads his Post-Gazette while the super drones on about
quotas and the problem with the temperature gauges and
the batches being too cold. What's there to hear that he
hasn't heard a million times already?

Give it a rest, Joe. O.H. 5 has been shut and gone for
20 years. Most people around here wouldn't know an
open hearth from a fireplace. Same with the Big Shop,
the Machine Shop, the 160" Plate Mill. All gone, Joe.
You should see the place now. Stores and parking lots.
Townhouses along the river. Can you imagine? But it's
not like what you're thinking, it's real nice, no more dirt
and noise. These townhouses are nothing like the shacks
that used to be down there, before they tore them down in
the '40s to expand the mill. Doctors and lawyers live there
now, folks with two dogs and no kids. What the hell do
they know about what went on here, how goddamn great
it was? About all that's left of the mill is the big plate press
in the middle of a parking lot. Twelve thousand tons of
steel. To big to move, so they put a little sign up and called
it historic. Hey, Joe, there's a coffee shop where you can
get a latte and a chocolate croissant.   Know what a latte
is, Joe? A croissant? See what I mean. It's not your world
anymore; the kids are all gone — Baltimore, New York,
Alaska. From the looks of your grave I bet none of them
ever visits with flowers.

You know what I'm going to do now, Joe? I'm going to get
away from all this sunlight and fresh air, drive down the
hill to Coral Lanes, sit with the cigarette smoke and stale
sweat-and-popcorn smell and listen to the balls roll down
the lanes. And I'll have a beer or two, Joe. After all these
years, just for you.

The Wheel

The dawn is filled with a glory of birds
erupting from the crowns of cottonwoods,
in spreading umbras of winged black,

And the man on the gravel path, lost
in thoughts of the day ahead, stops as

First one tree, then the next, and the next
through the meadow, west, along the creek,
explodes as the small black birds rise
to the blue spring morning, wheeling one way then

Another until before long a common
motion has been achieved so that one
great wheel circles overhead twice, sweeping
up stragglers, rising to greet the sun,
rising above the prairie, and only then moving away
and the man watches –

    So many birds!

    So many birds!

Stunned to thoughtless grace

—until they all disappear over the far houses
of his town, over the streets growing
with morning traffic, the human wheel forming,
turning, each with purpose, singular,
yet together, towards the day.

Like Old Buicks

A lone figure silhouetted in the fire of the rising sun, arms stretched overhead,
eager for the coming day. Before him lie mountains, dark outlines against the dawn.

****

Years as swift as swallows: I remember a beach, a woman, the impressions of our bodies in wet sand, washed away by the tide. Shells and water-smoothed glass.

My first sight of the Rockies — I was 19. For hours I strained to see mountains
and was fooled by clouds. Later, driving through Ten Sleep Canyon –
endless descent through switchbacks, snow on the high peaks, water below.

After she left I was lost. I should have seen it coming from a long way off, but like those mountains was tricked by what I hoped for, never saw what was right in front of me.
I tried living as a monk, a hillbilly hermit in the West Virginia hills. I read Zen, drank whiskey, grew turnips and potatoes. Didn't have the heart to shoot the groundhog who ate my peas and beans. Though largely I failed there — as farmer, monk and hermit — I think with great fondness of that farm. And because I lived off sacks of them, along with bacon, potatoes still remind me of West Virginia, even after all these years.

Sometimes it amazes me that I've lived as long as I have,

that my mind and body still work fairly well. I've gotten
where I am not, I'd like to think, by accident, but through
some greater design of which I'm only dimly aware. My life
has been, not unplanned, but rather full of plans, like cars
abandoned alongside country roads — large rusting Buicks
at least two decades old that once held dreams and lovers and
now are filled with snakes and the pale ghosts of desire.

I've always been good at reading maps, but get lost
nonetheless. Not lack of skill or attention, but an obstinate
humor that can't resist going wrong just to find out what
comes of it.

I've seen storm clouds breaking to reveal endless peaks,
watched the play of moonlight
on an alpine lake, chased a woman's smile across the country,
but missed much more
while staring down at my boots.

Tell me, do you think anyone will remember our sorrows and
joys,
when the earth has slept over us through a hundred winters?

For comfort, we have these, I hope they suffice:
a green leaf quivering in the noon sun, wind off a glacier and
fresh bear tracks.

And this: hills black against the sky when the sun has set,
hills we have walked that have watched over us as we passed.

Michael Adams

Spruce Mountain, West Virginia

I wanted this earth to speak through me,
to tell you – he tried to make a living
of it. It's true he failed, but there is no shame
in that. It takes more than a man and a woman,
and a small piece of land, to build something that endures.

You saw the farms scattered on the mountain,
the small towns of the valley –
         Onega, Seneca, Circleville, Cherry Grove

They may not look like much but by God
they have staying power. You don't enter
a place like this lightly. It takes generations
of blood and sweat flowing into the hardscrabble earth,
and not a little darkness.
The soil here is built of disappointment and fractured dreams.

Leave this land alone for a few years
and you may lose everything to its unassailable patience.
This thick woodland was once a meadow,
and the smell was not that of autumn leaves
and spring water, but the pungent odor of cow dung.
Here is where the house stood. You would have to get down
on your hands and knees now, a beggar, dig
in the damp earth to find any trace.
Someone must have carted off
the few things I left that were worth anything
before they set the fire. The rest is gone
to rust and the voracious creatures of the soil.

Look, there is the spring where we drew water,
next to it the big oak still stands, the one whose branches
sounded like small animals on the tin roof
when the wind blew in the autumn and the leaves were dry

but not yet fallen.

Right here was the kitchen where we would play
guitar and banjo and drink Jack Daniels straight up
until we were brave enough to venture
into the moonless November dark
to confront the mountain's
unhoused ghosts.

What words are fit to honor these mountains that rose
to heights unseen to this day, rose before
towering fern forests were locked in darkness
and began their ages-long decay
to the black rock we rend and gut this earth to find?

What words for these former Himalayas, softened by eons
of rain and the slow rafting of continents to today's tree-
green hills?

    I say there is wisdom here, solace, and much of the sacred.

What do our few decades matter?
Someday our remains will be scattered in a place
not unlike this, a place of trees and sky
and rough-hewn land, a part, finally, of it all.

I wanted this earth to speak as it does,
undeniable and unanswerable,
as the leaves, like the generations of men,
fall around us on this autumn day.

A man and woman and the great land.
Here for a season, for a few turnings
of the wheel to endure, to love,
to give what we can.
Then gone.

Sunnyside

Dolores and I drive the winding blacktop that hugs
Cement Creek, sunny May morning, coming down from
Gladstone and the Sunnyside Mine — all abandoned
now — back to Silverton. High above, the sun shines
on the slopes of Storm Peak, but we're at the bottom
of the valley, running through a dark boreal forest
of spruce and fir. Dolores points out the grade of
the old narrow-gauge railroad — built in the 1880s
— that served the mine, closed since the early 1990s,
last working silver mine in San Juan County, the rails
pulled up years ago, stacked like rusted cordwood at
the railroad station in town. Signs of bygone mining
days all around – falling down buildings, wood silvered
with age, holes in the hillsides, slate-blue tailing ponds,
and after a few moments of silence I say, those rails
might have been made where I grew up, Homestead,
Andrew Carnegie's steel works. Yes they were, Dolores
says, I saw Homestead stamped on the sides of the rails.
And then I see it, you never leave anything behind,
you take it all with you, think you've left the old mill
town, low green hills, the slow brown river, smoke and
stink, but it's all seeped into your pores and still with
you right here beside the fast mountain stream and
soaring peaks— the mills of Pennsylvania and mines of
Colorado, all tangled together. Carnegie built his mills,
fed them with the blood and dreams of men and women
brought by the boatload from Hungary, Slovakia,
Poland, Italy, Greece, Russia to the hell and hope and
struggle of America, a dollar a day, 12 hours, seven
days a week, a hundred dollars to the widows when
the men died in explosions, cave-ins, fell into vats of
molten metal. He fed it all to the furnaces and mines –
ore, coal and men. Crushed his workers with guns and
thugs and mind-numbing labor, made his fortune and

built a nation. Then he gave it all away.

I learned to swim in the basement of the Carnegie
Library in Homestead, fed my love of books there,
gazed up in awe at the Tyrannosaurus skeleton in the
Carnegie Museum in Pittsburgh, read there about the
Rocky Mountains and dreamed.   Now, all these years
later, I find a Carnegie Library in Silverton.

How we are shaped by land and water, the work
of a lifetime, nothing ever lost, Cement Creek, the
Monongahela River, everything carried along

> Silverton mines quiet, sinking
> by slow stages back into the earth,
> Homestead mills gone to weeds
> and failing memory.

> A dilapidated assay office,
> beside it, a rusted ore cart –
> filled with black soil
> and raspberry bushes.

Top of the World

My two companions and I have come up from
Cottonwood Creek to the knobbed spine of the Sangre
de Cristo Range. We're at 13,000 feet and far above
timberline. South, a knife-edge ridge of black rock
rises to Milwaukee Peak. North, the gentler flanks of
Marble Mountain. The San Luis Valley lies far below
to the west. We're walking a well-built trail of solid
stone riprap, but at the very crest of the ridge the trail
ends with no warning.

25 years ago I discovered that the maps of this area
were wrong, as maps of anything sometimes are, and
so had warned my companions. The old USGS 7.5
minute topo from 1955 shows a through trail down
into Sand Creek, and every map since – no matter
how new and improved, how many new vibrant colors,
how tearproof and waterproof, has faithfully recorded
the phantom trail. Faced now with a treacherous
descent down walls of loose rock and black ice-filled
gullies we marvel at the enduring work and we wonder
aloud, as I did a quarter-century past, about those
who built this trail with such care and effort, and why
they stopped here at the crest of the range.

Was it the young men of the Civilian Conservation
Corps
back in the '30s? It has
that look of solidity and optimism
found in so many works
of that time – the log lodges
of Yosemite and Yellowstone
that look as if they anchor the very earth
they stand upon,

The roads blasted from solid rock

    Serpent's Trail, Rim Rock Drive

shattering walls of poverty and despair.

There's something of the pride, even hubris, of the
Grand Coulee Dam in this trail.

America was a nation that faced it's troubles square
back then.
Hard, my God, how hard the times were
so many millions out of work,
broke, hungry, ragged and desperate.

They stood up, knew
how hard it was going to be,
that there was no choice
but sweat and hope and courage.

It was the time of the New Deal,
the square deal, a fair shake
for every ordinary man and woman.

Look at the pictures from those days –
Walker Evans and James Agee —

    Let Us Now Praise Famous Men

The bitter irony of that title.
They squint in black and white,
looking for a rain cloud in a white
washed out sky –
the hard lean women, ragged kids,
the men older at 30 than any of us
will ever be. Not a smile

anywhere. Tough,
it was tough.

And then, from the same years, the pictures
of the young men of the CCC,
from Detroit and Peoria,
Pittsburgh and Fresno,
hardscrabble Okies
and cool Brooklyn boys.

My father was one of them, building
roads and lodges in northern PA.
I have photos of him,
a cigarette dangling from lips set
in a half grin. A confident man,
hardly more than a boy and already fatherless,
standing with his arm around a buddy, both
of them leaning into each other
at the edge of a cliff –
a place called Top of the World –
nothing above but sky, and below –
trees and rock and the long drop
to the river.

Look at me boys, their faces seem to say.
Give me your best shot.
I can take it and give it back to you in spades.

I can imagine them here, 70 years ago, humping
the big iron bars, sledgehammers, hand drills and dynamite
on packstrings from the town of Crestone,
ten miles and 6,000' below,
just like John Henry, swinging the sledge
to drill a hole in the hard conglomerate,
pack it with blasting powder –

This here hammer rings like silver,
shines like gold, boys, shines like gold.

There were millions of them,
building roads, bridges, dams,
getting the country back on its feet.

I can see where the trail would have gone,
how the plans would have taken it down
gradually, in long contouring switchbacks,
see the cliffs to be blasted, the rock to be hauled.
They would have met right here
on the knife-edge of earth and sky.
There would have been celebratory pictures –
handshakes, arm wrestling,
hand stands on the summit of the world.

There were plans enough to put it on the maps but not on
        the ground.

Why did they stop here?
Was it for another project more critical – an amphitheater
amongst the towering red rocks
of Morrison, a road blasted from the cliffs
of the Colorado Plateau? Or was it
the War, a far darker and bloodier work?
After all this building, to destroy.
How many of these boys died under the steel rain
of Normandy, bled into the snows of Belgium, fell
from the skies, brought death to other boys as terrified as
they?

I won't travel that path now, imagine
those boys at that work, mowed down
like Colorado wheat, the nightmares and cold sweats
of the survivors, men like my father, living

the rest of his life on the far reach
of an unbridgeable divide, never again
the cocky young man of those early photos
taken before the War.

No, I won't travel that path,
but stay with them here in the mountains,
with the green-gray rock, its veins of gleaming
gray schist and black granite, and the delicate
purple wildflowers, with a clear
blue sky to the ends of the earth.

I'll stay with them here, try to conjure
something of their spirit, that spirit
that we need so badly now.

      We can do it, boys.
      All we need is three squares
      and a bunk.
      All we're asking is a fair shake.

             ****

Not long ago and not far from here
I came upon a crew of young men and women
at the same kind of work –
hard, hard, building a trail
at the top of the world.
They were dead serious
when serious was called for,
but they laughed with full laughter
and goofed and clowned at the creek
when the day's work was done.

I think back to those young people now,
offer them a silent thank you.
Backs grow weak, bodies old, but the spirit
lives on.

Ohio

Long green tunnel of oaks and maples,
branches arch overhead, a fine mist
fills the air.

Rhythmic crunch of shoes on gravel,
two pairs of feet keep the same beat.

Two brothers on the railroad grade,
and the minutes of their run flow
into years, back
to the sway of the cars,
click of steel wheels on rails,
a young boy's summer journey
from Pittsburgh to Ohio, the past a broad palette,
and in these timeless woods, the half century
that separates boy and man seems no more than a moment.

It's been well over thirty years
since the last train ran, and what was once
the Pennsylvania and Lake Erie line
is now the Headwaters Trail.

The station master on the platform
with his yellow flag waving
up and down to signal the engineer
to stop and pick up passengers
is long dead and the train station —
windows shuttered, paint peeling, roof
losing its battle with
rain, wind and sun —
is a ghost ship from another time,
stranded on the shoals of a world falling
endlessly into the future.

The woods in their timeless now,
two middle-aged men, spring,
the long embrace of the earth.

Green Chili

Start with 4 or 5 slices of bacon
in a cast iron Dutch oven, low heat.
Remove while still soft, retaining the grease.
Cube a pound of pork and toss it in.

Sprinkle in just enough
whole wheat flour to coat the meat
and soak up the fat, brown thoroughly,
add water and red wine and simmer.

Pour yourself a glass of that wine—
it's 18 degrees, 20" of snow already
fallen and it's still curtaining down.
It's three days 'til Christmas, your wife's
in New York and maybe she'll be back
tomorrow, but today no one is going anywhere.

Might as well enjoy a good Merlot.

When the wine has cooked down, open
a jar of stewed tomatoes, pour
the juice into the pot and then, one by one,
tear the thick red fruit apart with your hands.

You may make a mess –
        the pure tactile joy of it—
        juice and seeds squirting everywhere –
It's not the first time
and it certainly won't be the last.

Do you remember those warm August evenings
in the garden, the aroma of tomato leaves trailing
your hands into the house, how you would press them
gently against her cheeks and she would draw

a long breath and exhale summer?

There are gardens in the face of war, defiant
gardens, celery grown
    in the trenches, smell of basil mixed with
mustard gas.
    In the ghettos, the camps, the front lines,
greenness is the dream scenery
    of those refusing damnation, hope in the face of
death.

Pull a piece of pork from the pot. If it falls apart in
your mouth, you're ready to go on.

Chop a large onion and 5 or 6 cloves of garlic,
sauté in a separate skillet
until the flesh of the onion becomes translucent.
Add to the meat and –
    oh, yes, I almost forgot –
add the bacon, too. Eat one piece, chop
up the rest and toss it in.   Then dried mustard,
turmeric,
a little salt, fennel and black pepper. And cilantro –
it will be dried not fresh, but some things can't be helped.

You've got Tom Waits on the stereo — you've
been listening all day to Orphans, the three disc set your
brother sent you, and now you're filled with love for
your brother, you want to call him and tell him but of
course you don't, you and he don't do that sort of thing.
You send each other music, like this gravel-voiced
genius that your wife hates – absolutely can't stand his
voice, the sacrilege of him singing Frank Sinatra – but
you and your brother love it, and now Tom is singing
Down There by the Train, and you sing along as you stir
the chili, sing about a train whose whistle can be heard

"from the halls of Heaven to the gates of Hell", where
every sin is forgiven, every sinner washed clean, and
you want to believe that the forsaken can be saved, you
want to hear that whistle, alone in your house two days
before Christmas, missing her, cooking for someone not
there, you want to believe in spite of yourself that you
and the whole world can hear that whistle and ride that
train.

And so this chili, because you do believe that there is no
greater act of love, no greater faith than to cook and to
feed someone else.

Now for the peppers, one large can
of Rio Grande chili peppers, chopped
medium fine. Then the last
of the jalapeno and serrano peppers chopped very fine—
the ones that you picked the evening
before the first hard frost of October,
breathing the sharp autumn air, and as you carried them
into the house, stopped and looked up at the Summer
        Triangle,
recited the names
    —

     Vega   Deneb   Altair

     As we ruin ourselves in the stupidity of another
war, think of pepper plants
        and the tiny white flowers that herald the fruit,
how something so delicate
        holds the promise of fire.

Leave the lid off and let it cook down.

Another glass of wine. This snowfall

is a sacrament and you're getting drunk.
Go out onto the back deck,
let the falling snow dampen your hair.
After the heat and closeness of the kitchen,
you need to breathe for a minute or two.

Back inside, the chili's aroma is rich and heavy, too
complex
for you to pick out the web of smells beneath the wine and
pork.
Try it. Almost there, maybe a little dried habanero
and a touch more dried mustard.
Not too hot, though, that would be to your taste, not
hers.

What light the sun has brought today is fading
and yet there is a blue-white radiance, as some cold fire,
emanating from within the fallen snow.

You miss her – the space her body
occupies and the hot flesh itself. Desire
does not fade with the years and your
rough hands are greedy to fit themselves
to the curves of her flanks, to feel her need
respond to your own.

The world may be going to hell –
inevitably and always – and one day you will be gone.
But what of it? As long as a man can cook
because he wants to feed a woman, because
he wants to please her, there's hope for the world.
Take this wine and drink your fill.
Take this chili, this stew
of the earth's bounty, and eat.

Autumn Night: Cold Mountain

1.
Late at night, I rise,
sleep distant, leave
the long body of my wife
to her dreams for the company
of Han Shan and Shih Te.

Rain drips from the eaves,
though the moon is out,
washing the trees in bone-light.

So many sorrows in this life,
so many joys!

I would leap the bounds of the earth,
sit with the moon among clouds.

2.
2AM and sleepless,
 I rise to the autumn darkness.
Outside, streetlights swim,
drunken sailors
in the rain.

I make coffee, embrace
the long body of night.

3.
The first rain of autumn wakes me.
I am unable to return to sleep.
My lover lies next to me,
warm and content.

STEEL VALLEY

I think of Cold Mountain and long
to leap the world's ties,
sit with him amongst the clouds.

I place my hand on the warm lands
of my lover, wander her hills and valleys.

Tears fill my eyes.

Cherry Tree

The cherry tree where she waited,
bird-crowned amidst a storm
of pink blossoms –

Barren now beneath the December sky.

Generations of songbirds have passed,
their tiny bones and brave hearts
one with earth and sky

Where is she now?

Her soft brown hair
white
as the winter's snow.

Apples

I'm leaning against my truck at the farmer's market
in Louisville, Colorado eating an apple — a small,
firm, very tart Jonathan. The market's just a tent
and a refrigerated truck in the parking lot of a small
shopping center. You know the kind of place, you find
them everywhere these days — eight years ago it was
alfalfa fields and pasture, now there are a couple of
restaurants, a liquor store, doggie boutique, and a coffee
shop. I stop here at least a couple of times a week and,
if it's not busy, spend 10 or 15 minutes talking to the
farmer. He's in his 30s and passionately dedicated to
organic farming. You have to be, to make a living at it
in the Boulder Valley, on the northern edge of Denver's
rapidly growing metropolitan area of 3 million. Still,
there's a strong demand for fresh organic produce here,
and so he scrapes by, and for that I'm glad and give him
as much business as I can.

The apple I'm eating is deep purple-red and small, the
size of a large plum, but what does size matter? The
right apple can give you the whole world — the tang,
bite and zest of it, the strong sweet rot of an abandoned
orchard in November, a May blizzard of apple
blossoms, the salt and sweet of a girl's lips at a first kiss.
And it's best enjoyed out-of-doors, with wind and sun
or rain or the smell of sweat and wet leaves. In *Wild
Apples*, written a few months before his untimely death
in May of 1862, Henry Thoreau wrote, "To appreciate
the wild and sharp flavors of these October fruits, it is
necessary that you be breathing the sharp October or
November air." Of wild apples, he said, "Some of these
apples may be labeled, 'To be eaten in the wind."

I'm on my way home from work, I'm tired and I smell

bad, not the honest odor of physical labor, but the kind of funky smell you get from too many meetings and sitting in front of a computer all day, never getting outdoors. It wasn't a bad day; it wasn't a good day, but it's over now, the work part. It's October and the mountains to the west – the Indian Peaks, Longs Peak, the Mummy Range — have a dusting of new snow that fell last night. It's warm and sunny now, but a solid bank of black clouds is moving down fast from the northwest, and when it gets here I know it will bring wind and cold. It looks like I have 5 or 10 minutes to enjoy the sun, no more. But I'm looking forward to the coming of the front and the change it will bring, the blast of wind coming from the west, moving through the trees like a breaking wave, the sharp clean smell of rain.

This apple is good, but the best ones are wild, from a tree long abandoned and forgotten by all but the deer and the wanderer, returned to its own true nature, what Thoreau called "the Saunterer's Apple – you must lose yourself before you can find the way to that." One of life's great gifts is to be offered such an apple when you're still young enough for that magic when the whole earth turns around a single moment and what comes after is different from what came before. For me it was the hills of western Pennsylvania, a late September afternoon in 1970, just shy of my 21st year. My girl and I had ridden down the Youghiogheny River, south of Pittsburgh, through the old coal mining district with the beehive coke ovens dug into the hillsides, through towns that had sunk into a long senescence years before — Dawson, Broadford, Connellsville – towns with narrow potholed streets, many of brick or cobblestone, quiet and nearly deserted downtowns, and modest frame houses sided in asphalt that crowd the street. South of Connellsville we left the river and rode up into the

mountains, up Chestnut Ridge and into the Laurel
Highlands, our ancient BMW motorcycle sputtering
on the steep grades. The hills were ablaze with the
red of maple trees and the gold of oaks. We chose the
narrowest, least traveled roads we could find. The tree
branches made a tunnel over our heads and the wheels
of the bike kicked up leaves as we passed and swirled
them around us, so that there was a continuous play of
light and shadows and flashing golds and reds to mark
our passage. We had our sleeping bags, a block of white
cheese, loaf of whole wheat bread, and a half gallon of
cheap red wine, the screw-top variety – we were damn
poor but always managed to scrape together enough
cash for gas for the bike and wine for our souls – and
we pulled off onto an overgrown lane. The sun was high
and warm. At the end of the lane was an abandoned
orchard. The apples were green and no larger than a
baby's fist. We drank a couple of tin cups full of wine
and started eating the apples. They were so tart they
pulled the moisture right out of our mouths, and we had
to screw our eyes shut and wrinkle our faces like prunes
to eat them, but we had a nice buzz on and even with
the tartness there was a touch of sweetness and a spice
like nutmeg and cloves that I couldn't get enough of.
Or maybe it was her, she was everything to me in those
days. God, we had plans. We were going places, Karen
and I. I was in my last year of college; she was a junior.
We would both graduate with degrees in anthropology.
Maybe there would be graduate school somewhere
down the line, but for the immediate future I'd work for
a year and then, after she graduated we'd buy a camper
van, travel up to New Hampshire to pick apples for the
harvest and then drive down the east coast and winter
along the Gulf. After that, on to California. It didn't
work out that way, and I haven't seen her in 30 years. I
hope she's doing well. When I eat tart green apple I still

taste the cool moist of her lips, the hint of cinnamon in
her breath.

After we'd eaten one or two, she said, the seeds have
cyanide, you know. I said, watch. That was when I
learned how to eat an apple, the way I do it to this
day. Make your first bite from the bottom, the small
indentation where the blossom was, then eat all around
the core until you reach the stem. Place the core in
your mouth; suck the remaining flesh from it. Savor
the tartness you find there. Then bite down. Enjoy the
bitterness of the seeds, a little poison, along with the
sweetness, to remind you of what life holds in store.
And equally a reminder of the heart's innate resilience,
that it can bear some poison and still beat strong.

The wind rises, the air fills with a blizzard of leaves,
and the wall of dark clouds blocks the sun. Hard, cold
drops of rain sting my face. I stay in the wind and rain
while I finish the apple. I chew the last of the core into
pulp, swallow it, then climb back into my truck. The
taste stays with me all the way home.

A Train Will Take You

...and I hear far off in the sense of coming night that
engine calling our mountains
                                        —Jack Kerouac

A train will take you out of yourself, into the ever
falling curve of the earth, the star-washed rivers and
the flowing hills, and the tractor dust of the prairies
and corn-green farms of the prairies, and the cold
streets and hot jazz nights of the cities. Maybe you're
in the lounge car, feet up on the windowsill, watching
the Colorado River, the long climb upstream to the
headwaters, sage brush to pine to the tall snow-sculpted
spruce, and the snow shining on the peaks in the
evening light. And the train stops in Fraser in the cool
evening air for a smoke break, the smokers in clusters,
talking or silent under the first bright stars, as you and
your woman walk along the train, smelling the mixed
smells of diesel and cigarettes and the saw-mill smell of
fresh cut wood until the whistle blows everyone back
into the cars for the night run into Denver. And now
you've crossed the Continental Divide into the June
night of east-flowing waters, and your sleeping wife's
head gentle on your shoulder, the rails rocking you
now down towards the great flat plains, and you sway
through a tunnel to the big rush of sky and there are the
lights of Denver, small against the night and the endless
rolling grasslands, and you're pulled out of yourself, a
heart and soul and part of the big land. And the land
calls you and the swift mountain creeks of trout, the
slow brown rivers of herons and farms, calls you down
the South Platte to the Platte, across Nebraska, the
Missouri and the lands of the Mandan and Sioux and
trappers, the hard times of the Dust Bowl, the stars
bright and close. Here you are on a train, in love with

a woman and the breathing of her breath and here you are, too, on the Mark Twain Mississippi, the broad black of the river, blacker than the sky, and the bars and chemical plants and music of St. Louis, down now through the heart of America, your country, stupid and beautiful, it tears your heart out, how you love it, cruel and ugly and as kind and generous as the world all at once.

And the train runs out of the mountains, sheds the close breathing of pines for the big night sky, picks up speed on the flat run across the prairie and into Denver. Your heart's far to the east, though, on the Ohio of barges and the mills of Wheeling, and the families of Marietta and Liverpool secure in their beds and the homeless under the salt-stained bridges and the rich criminals in their gated mansions and the working mothers with their clapboard rowhouse children, and the low heartbreak HOOOO of a tug pushing a train of coke barges as the pilot blows his horn coming down from Pittsburgh. Back up now through the old green hill-steep valleys of youth, the houses and long wooden stairs climbing the hills, past the scarred coal towns and into the old rolling mountains of youth. Chestnut Ridge, Allegheny Mountain, the rock-swift streams, the aching beauty of dogwood and mountain laurel blossoms high on a stony ridge. And your heart, with its yearning bigger than the years, and its dreams fulfilled or broken or still to come, settling now as the train slows beneath the highways, a light rain falling, switching past the graveyards of buses and the blank warehouses of late night Denver, the weedy margins of train yards and the rain-black puddles of gravel and weeds, and into Union Station, and you nudge your wife gently awake and tell her, here we are.

Notes

Monongahela

Monongahela is an Algonquian word meaning "high banks falling down".

Steel

"goddam Hunky troublemaker": While the 1919 steel strike had almost universal support amongst both skilled and unskilled steelworkers in Chicago and Gary, in the Pittsburgh area – especially in Homestead and Braddock – support was confined to Slovak steelworkers, who made up the great majority of unskilled laborers. The Slovaks were viewed by native-born steelworkers as dangerous radicals and were referred to by the racial epithet of "Hunky".

Black Cossacks

In the early 20th century the Pennsylvania Coal and Iron Police, later the State Police, hated and feared by labor, were referred to as the "Black Cossacks."

The Valley

The Monongahela Valley, or Steel Valley, was the most heavily industrialized river valley in the world in the first half of the 20th century.

Youghiogheny is an Algonquian word meaning "contrary stream".

Homestead Blues

Joe Magarac was the Paul Bunyan of steel. Magarac means "donkey" in Croatian and Joe was the big-hearted, hard-working hero of eastern European immigrants in southwestern Pennsylvania. Joe could bend bars of red-hot steel with his bare hands and always had a helping hand to lend. John Henry was a historic figure, a black convict laborer who helped build the Big Bend tunnel on the C&O Railroad in West Virginia in the 1870s. John Henry's battle against the steam drill, an epic struggle of man against machine, has become an American legend.

Where We Come From
"the reek of dead fish rises": In 1983 protests occurred in mill towns up and down the Monongahela against Mellon Bank after the bank foreclosed on Mesta Machine in West Homestead. Mesta was a major employer in the region and manufactured tools and dies for the steel industry. The most notorious protests began in Monessen when steelworkers entered the Mellon Bank branch. One group of steelworkers distracted the tellers by changing five dollars bills for rolls of pennies while another group quietly walked to safe deposit boxes they had rented previously and deposited dead fish. When the bank was opened the next morning the smell was overwhelming.

Sunnyside
Andrew Carnegie's Homestead Steel Works manufactured over half of the steel rails made in the United States in the last decades of the 19th century.

Michael Adams grew up in a steel town near Pittsburgh, PA. He has a B.A. in Anthropology and a Master's degree in planning, both from the University of Pittsburgh. He is the author of five books of poetry and essays, including *Broken Hand Peak* (Turkey Buzzard Press, 2008) *Underground* (Longhand Press, 2007) and *Between Heaven and Earth* (Elik Press, 2004). *Whistleblowers* (Turkey Buzzard Press 2009) is his most recent work, like *Underground* a collaboration with the poets James Taylor III and Phil Woods. These three poets perform together as the **Free Radical Railroad**. Michael is the winner of the 2007 Mark Fischer Poetry Prize, awarded by the Telluride Writers Guild. He now lives in Lafayette, CO with his wife, Claire.

Publication Credits

Between Heaven and Earth (Elik Press, Salt Lake City, Utah 2003)

Singing This Great Body Back Together (Baculite Publishing, Columbine Hills, CO 2002) (editor)

Hardscrabble: The Wet Mountain Poems (Longhand Press, Golden, CO 1997)

Broken Hand (Longhand Press 1991)

Underground (Longhand Press, 2007) A collaboration with poets Phil Woods and James Taylor III

Broken Hand Peak (reprint of the title poem from Broken Hand) (Turkey Buzzard Press, Lafayette, CO 2007)

Whistleblowers (Turkey Buzzard Press 2009)

Poetry, fiction, book reviews and essays have appeared in numerous magazines, journals and newspapers, including *Mad Blood* (Evergreen, CO), *Mountain Gazette* (Frisco, CO), *San Juan Mountain Journal* (Silverton, CO), *Northern Lights* (Missoula, MT), *Pilgrimage* (Crestone, CO), *Desert Shovel* (Santa Fe. NM), *Heartlodge* (Denver, CO), *Hiram Poetry Review* (Hiram, OH), *Bombay Gin* (Boulder, CO), *Midwest Quarterly* (Pittsburg, KS), *Alabama Literary Review* (Troy, AL), and Writers on the Range, a syndication service of High Country News (Paonia, CO).

Awards

Winner of the 2007 Mark Fischer Poetry Prize awarded by the Telluride Writers' Guild for the poem *Still, We Have the Birds*

ABOUT LUMMOX PRESS

LUMMOX Press was created in 1994 by RD Armstrong. It began as a self-publishing/DIY imprint for poetry by RD. Several chapbooks were published and in late 1995 it began publishing the LUMMOX Journal, a monthly small/underground press lit-arts zine. Available primarily by subscription, the LJ continued it's exploration of the "creative process" until its demise as a print mag in 2006.

During its eleven year existence, this tiny mag with the big name, interviewed poets, musicians and artists (over 100 in all) about how they do what they do. Hundreds of poems were also published in its pages. Poets like *Todd Moore, Lyn Lifshin, Gerald Locklin, Holly Prado, L.A. Bogen, Linda Lerner, Scott Wannberg, Philomene Long, John Thomas* and *RD Armstrong,* to name a few, appeared regularly within its pages. It was hailed as one of the best monthly's in the small press.

In 1998, LUMMOX began publishing the Little Red Book series, and continues to do so today. To date there are some 63 titles in the series (as of 2009) and this year a collection of poems from the first decade of the series has been published under the title, The Long Way Home (2009).

LUMMOX has published the following titles: The Wren Notebook by Rick Smith (2000); Last Call: The Legacy of Charles Bukowski (2004); Fire and Rain – Selected Poems 1993-2007 Volumes 1 & 2 by RD Armstrong (2008); On/Off the Beaten Path (a trio of long poems about road trips taken in 1999, 2000 and 2001 including the epic poem RoadKill – which John Berbrich said was "the best post 9-11 writing I've seen") by RD Armstrong (2008); El Pagano and Other Twisted Tales (a collection of short stories and flash fiction) by RD Armstrong (2008); New and Selected Poems by John Yamrus (2008); The Riddle of the Wooden Gun by Todd Moore (2009); Sea Trails by Pris Campbell (2009); Down This Crooked Road – Modern Poetry from the Road Less Traveled edited by RD Armstrong and William Taylor, Jr. (2009); Drive By – Shards & poems by John Bennett; Modest Aspirations by Gerald Locklin (poems) and Beth Wilson (stories) (2010). These books are available directly from the LUMMOX Press via the website: www. lummoxpress.com or at Lummox c/o PO Box 5301 San Pedro, CA 90733. There are also E-Book versions of most titles available. You can also buy them via major online sellers...

* * *

Together with Chris Yeseta (Layout and Art Direction since 1997), RD continues to publish books that are both striking in their looks as well as their content...

Please visit the website to read selections from these titles as well as peruse the many other titles/ articles published by the LUMMOX Press.

www.ingramcontent.com/pod-product-compliance
Lightning Source LLC
Chambersburg PA
CBHW020921090426
42736CB00008B/742